SENTENCE TYPES and PUNCTUATION

ANN RIGGS

CREATIVE C EDUCATION

Published by Creative Education
P.O. Box 227, Mankato, Minnesota 56002
Creative Education is an imprint of The Creative Company
www.thecreativecompany.us

Design and production by Liddy Walseth
Art direction by Rita Marshall
Printed by Corporate Graphics in the United States of America

Photographs by Alamy (Photos 12), Art Resource (The Andy Warhol Foundation, Inc.), Corbis
(Fritz Hoffmann/In Pictures, Swim Ink 2, LLC), Getty Images (Ben Cranke, Dorling Kindersley, GK Hart/Vikki
Hart, Hulton Archive, Kurt Hutton/Picture Post, Mansell/Time & Life Pictures, Mercury Archives,
H. Armstrong Roberts, Joel Sartore/National Geographic, Kim Taylor, Lisa Valder, Gandee Vasan), iStockphoto
(Jill Battaglia, James Brey, Eric Isselée, Stefan Klein, Kevin Klopper, Sean Locke, Ray Roper, Duncan Walker)

Page 28 illustration by Etienne Delessert

Library of Congress Cataloging-in-Publication Data
Riggs, Ann.
Sentence types and punctuation / by Ann Riggs.
p. cm. — (Understanding grammar)
Includes bibliographical references and index.
Summary: An examination of the rules behind English grammar, focusing on the
components known as sentences and punctuation, whose various forms and types provide
the fundamental structures of writing.
ISBN 978-1-60818-095-0
1. English language—Sentences. 2. English language—Punctuation. 3. English
language—Grammar. I. Title. II. Series.

PE1439.R54 2010
428.2—dc22   2010028299

CPSIA: 110310PO1386

First Edition
2 4 6 8 9 7 5 3 1

TABLE of CONTENTS

Music swells. Siblings squabble. Owls hoot. I am. Grammar is. And just like

that, two words can become a SENTENCE. The information in a short sentence can be

expanded by adding more words that give vivid descriptions or specific reactions.

Where should those words be placed? How does a writer know what PUNCTUATION to

use? What does all of that mean, anyway? Words fall into place more easily when

one has an understanding of grammar, a system of rules that gives writers the foun-

dation for producing acceptable, formal expression. It is that acceptable form, that

appropriate grammar, which helps readers comprehend what has been written.

But why do we call it a *sentence*? Since the 12th century A.D., our vocabulary has

been influenced by our Latin-speaking ancestors; their word *sentire* means "to feel,

be of the opinion." Basic sentences have a subject (someone or something) and a

PREDICATE or verb (action or state of being). Each complete thought means something

because of the individual words that comprise it and the punctuation that defines

its limits. A sentence begins with a capital letter and concludes with an end mark,

which can be a period, a question mark, or an exclamation point. The ending punc-

tuation mark indicates to the reader if a group of words conveys a statement, a command, a question, or an exclamation. Other punctuation helps specify whether the sentences consist only of a MAIN CLAUSE or a combination of a main and one or more SUBORDINATE CLAUSES.

Does that sound complicated? It doesn't need to be. Writers depend on end punctuation marks as well as other symbols, such as commas, semicolons, colons, dashes, hyphens, apostrophes, quotation marks, and parentheses, to help their writing make sense. The word "punctuation" has its Latin root in *punctuat*, meaning "brought to a point." That's the goal, to bring the reader to the conclusion—the point—that you want to make, and punctuation gives you an accepted, reliable way to communicate. Knowing more about words helps you write better sentences; knowing more about sentences and punctuation helps you make your point most clearly.

SENSIBLE SENTENCES

Knowing the different kinds of sentences and how they function can help you decide what kind of sentence to write. There are four basic types: declarative, interrogative, imperative, and exclamatory. A declarative sentence makes a statement and ends with a period. This is the most frequently used sentence type, and it states a fact or an argument without asking the reader to do anything about it. Consider the following examples: **The previous sentences were declarative. Using spell-check on a computer doesn't eliminate a writer's need to carefully proofread.** Both are simple statements of fact.

An interrogative sentence is different. It asks a direct question of its reader, expecting an answer. Interrogative sentences always end with a question mark, as in: **What time will you get home from the dance?** An indirect question, however, is merely a statement and should not be confused with the direct questions posed by interrogative sentences. In the sentence, **She asked what had happened to the containers with melted ice cream in them,** no one is doing the asking—the event is just being recorded as a statement, making it a declarative sentence. Like declarative sentences, imperative sentences usually end with a period. Unlike declarations, though, the subject (you) is understood, and an imperative gives a command or makes a request, as in **Read Chapter 17 for Tuesday's quiz.** An exclamatory sentence is a complete statement with strong feeling that ends with an exclamation point: **LuAnn scored five goals in the soccer game!** To emphasize a particularly strong feeling, as in the called an , you may also use an exclamation point, as in **hey!** or **oh!**

Novelists, such as American author Catherine Marshall (1914–83), use a variety of sentence types, as Marshall's 1967 book about a 19-year-old teacher named Christy Huddleston shows. *Christy* tells the story of a city girl who finds herself totally unprepared to teach the impoverished children of a small community in the Appalachian Mountains and of her interactions with residents such as the young, local minister, Mr. Grantland. Try to identify all four types of sentences in the following passage describing Christy's first day at school:

HEY!
OH!

Looking back I can see that the young walk unabashedly into many a situation that the more experienced would avoid at all costs. Not that I was cocky or overconfident that first day of school. The truth was that I was trying hard to settle the butterflies in my stomach so that Mr. Grantland would think me an experienced teacher....

For this first day of school [Grantland] had put away his working clothes and was dressed in a tweed suit with a white shirt and bow tie. His only concession to the snow was heavy boots laced almost to his knees....

"Is this a fashion parade on Fifth Avenue?" His voice was teasing. "Those are silly, silly shoes. Ice-pick toes."

"I know."

"Hold on! Steady!" he exclaimed as I slipped....

The yard was swarming with children waiting for the first glimpse of their new teacher. Most were flaxen-haired, skinny, too pale, none dressed warmly enough for January. Some were climbing over the piles of lumber and rocks in the yard, some running in and out of the building, their high-pitched voices ringing in the clear air. What if I could not handle such lively pupils? ...

Seeing us coming, the children had stopped whatever they were doing to stare at me. As we got closer, I saw with a shock that many of them were barefooted. I knew that some had to walk several miles in the snow. Suddenly I was painfully self-conscious about my foolish shoes. Their bare feet made me want to tuck my own feet out of sight to hide the tokens of my vanity. What a lot I had to learn!

Most of the 21 sentences in this excerpt are statements, which is often the case in NARRATION. Did you find 16 declarative sentences? In a tone more declarative than anything else, the author describes the setting through the eyes of the apprehensive, novice teacher. We read Christy's descriptions of Mr. Grantland and of the students and learn what her first impressions of them are. Two interrogative sentences, well-placed to interrupt the teacher's thoughts, offer a clue to Grantland's personality and to Christy's uncertainty about her own abilities. Then when she slips in the snow, Grantland's two imperatives, *Hold on! Steady!*, jolt both Christy and the reader, who perhaps begins empathizing with the teacher's plummeting confidence. But the clincher of the excerpt comes in the final exclamatory sentence, when she realizes that she isn't fooling anyone with her appearance, least of all herself. Through their differences, the four kinds of sentences work together to effectively set the scene early in the book. What would we have missed if all the sentences had been declarative? Without questions, commands, and exclamations, conversations and stories themselves can lose their

HOLD ON! STEADY!

flavor. A good writer knows when to use each type of sentence to get the right effect.

BUILD YOUR OWN SENTENCE
Sibling Rivalry Sentences

The following excerpt from American novelist Louisa May Alcott's (1832–88) classic, *Little Women* (1868), contains all four sentence types: declarative, imperative, interrogative, and exclamatory. Copy Amy and Jo's conversation on paper, then label each sentence's type. Carefully reproduce all punctuation as well.

"Come, Jo, it's time."

"For what?"

"You don't mean to say you have forgotten that you promised to make half a dozen calls with me today?"

"I've done a good many rash and foolish things in my life, but I don't think I ever was mad enough to say I'd make six calls in one day, when a single one upsets me for a week."

"Yes, you did; it was a bargain between us. I was to finish the crayon of Beth for you, and you were to go properly with me, and return our neighbors' visits.... It's a lovely day, no prospect of rain, and you pride yourself on keeping promises; ... Jo March, you are perverse enough to provoke a saint!"

Louisa May Alcott

ANSWER KEY

Sentence types given in order of appearance: imperative, interrogative, interrogative, declarative, declarative, declarative, declarative, exclamatory

FROM SIMPLE TO COMPLEX

The four types of sentences can take on four different forms: simple, compound, complex, and compound-complex. The most basic sentence structure is the simple sentence. It contains one subject and one verb. As a matter of fact, the previous two sentences were examples of simple sentences. In the first, "structure" is the subject, and "is" serves as the verb. In the second, "It" is the subject, while "contains" is the verb. Additional words were used as MODIFIERS, PREDICATE NOMINATIVES, and OBJECTS, but the structure of each sentence was based on one subject and one verb.

Furthermore, we can say that a simple sentence is made up of a single clause, and the definition for both a sentence and a "clause" remains the same: each is a group of words with a subject and a verb. An independent clause can stand alone—it makes sense all by itself. Consider the following sentence: **An independent clause doesn't depend upon other words.** From declarative to exclamatory, a simple sentence can be any type and any length. In the simple, one-word exclamatory sentence **Help!** an understood subject (you) and an exclamation point at the end grab the reader's attention. And a simple declarative sentence makes a statement, even if it takes many words to do it: **Wishing away the blustery January afternoon, Tina propped herself up on the couch pillows and daydreamed about summertime.** The complete subject is longer in this sentence

(*Wishing away the blustery January afternoon, Tina*), and the complete predicate has a few more words than some simple sentences do (*propped herself up on the couch pillows and daydreamed about summertime*), but there is still only one subject and one verb, even though the verb has two parts and is connected by "and": Tina propped and daydreamed. The two verbs joined by "and" make a compound verb, but the sentence category is still simple, since "Tina" is the only subject.

Not to be confused with compound verbs, a compound sentence has two or more independent clauses joined by words known as coordinating conjunctions that help the clauses work together—that coordinate them. In the case of a compound sentence, two or more equal, independent clauses are joined by a coordinating conjunction such as *and*, *but*, *or*, *for*, *nor*, *yet*, and sometimes *so*. A comma ends the first of the two independent clauses, and the coordinating conjunction begins the second clause. Compounds are ideal when comparing or contrasting situations, as in **Herb got out of bed when his alarm rang, *and* he had plenty of time to get ready for school.** Here's another example: **The bus was on time, *but* Wanda wasn't.**

The danger in making compound sentences is that they can be overused, become over-connected, and get out of balance. Think about how an excited child might tell about her day at the park.

AND BUT OR FOR NOR YET SO

 We went to the park today, and we fed the ducks and the geese and the squirrels, but some of them were kind of shy and didn't come as close to us as the ducks did, and then we got to see some of the geese fly away.

This is a grammatically correct sentence. The problem with it is that, even though there are commas and coordinating conjunctions, the writing sounds like a child's. Unless that is the writer's intent, it needs to be rewritten. In fact, the compound sentence form may not be the best choice for integrating all of that information, either.

Perhaps the complex form is what we should use to convey our adventure in the park. A complex sentence is a combination of independent and dependent clauses. As its name implies, the dependent clause needs help; it can't stand alone. Another term for a dependent clause is sentence fragment, because it is only a piece, or fragment, of a complete thought. As a rule, fragments are unacceptable in most formal written work because they are not complete sentences. Clues for recognizing dependent clauses are the words, called subordinating conjunctions, that introduce them: *after*, *although*, *as*, *because*, *before*, *how*, *if*, *once*, *since*, *than*, *that*, *then*, *though*, *till*, *until*, *when*, *where*, *whether*, and *while*. If we began the first sentence in the above example with a subordinating conjunction and alter the rest like so, ***When* we went to the park today, we fed the ducks and geese but not the shy squirrels**, we would achieve a complex sentence with a dependent clause followed by an independent clause.

Now that we have an understanding of compound and complex sentences, the next step is to see the two combined. Merging two independent clauses, two thoughts that can stand alone, with at least one dependent clause that can't gives us another form. Let's go back to the ducks and geese, rewording a bit, and illustrate the new kind of sentence: ***When* the shy squirrels found us, we tried to feed them, too, *even though* we had really planned to feed only the geese and ducks, *and* we had only a little bit of bread.** The *when* clause is a clue for dependency. So is the *even though* part of the sentence that is set off by commas. Two other clauses are independent: **we tried to feed them, too** and **we had only a little bit of bread**. Although these clauses don't need any help, they are further explained by the rest of the sentence. Combining two independent clauses (compound sentence form) with the dependent clauses makes the sentence form compound-complex. From simple subjects and verbs to compound-complex mind-benders, sentences can take on a variety of structures, each with its own purpose. As a writer, your job is to pick the form that best fits your subject, and use each clause to your advantage.

In Complete Control

Why do you think some people are attracted to perilous sports, such as skydiving, snowboarding, and kayaking or other dangerous activities, such as racing motorcycles, skateboarding, or mountain climbing? Curiosity? Bravery? To impress others? To endure pain? To make money?

To prove something to themselves or others? Perhaps it just takes a special kind of person. What skills are required? Write your answer without using sentence fragments (as was intentionally done in the above words and phrases) in at least seven complete sentences, each with its own subject and verb, taking care to support your argument with specific examples.

VARIOUS INTERPRETATIONS

G ood writers strive for variety in sentence form and function. American humorist James Thurber (1894–1961) employs two compound, four complex, and two compound-complex sentences in the following excerpt from Michael J. Rosen's *The Dog Department: James Thurber on Hounds, Scotties, and Talking Poodles* (2001). Pay particular attention to the sentence parts.

"Speaking of puppies, as I was a while back, I feel that I should warn inexperienced dog owners who have discovered to their surprise and dismay a dozen puppies in a hall closet or under the floor of the barn, not to give them away. Sell them or keep them, but don't give them away. Sixty percent of persons who are given a dog for nothing bring him back sooner or later and plump him into the reluctant and unprepared lap of his former owner. The people say that they are going to Florida and can't take the dog, or that he doesn't want to go; or they point out that he eats first editions or lace curtains or spinets; or that he doesn't see eye to eye with them in the matter of housebreaking; or that he makes disparaging remarks under his breath about their friends. Anyway, they bring him back and you are stuck with him—and maybe six others. But if you charge ten or even five dollars for pups, the new owners don't dare return them. They are afraid to ask for their money back because they believe you might think they are hard up and need the five or ten dollars. Furthermore, when a mischievous puppy is returned to its former owner it invariably behaves beautifully, and the person who brought it back is likely to be regarded as an imbecile or a dog-hater or both.

Let's investigate a few of Thurber's sentences. The following dependent clauses appear in the first sentence: **as I was a while back; that I should warn inexperienced dog-owners not to give them away; who have discovered to their surprise and dismay a dozen puppies in a hall closet or under the floor of the barn**. Sometimes, as it does here, the RELATIVE PRONOUN *who* acts as a subject of a dependent clause. But none of those groups of

I FEEL

words is an independent clause, even though each has a subject and a verb. Imagine that: the only independent clause in the whole sentence, **I feel**, is only two words! That's one complex sentence.

Notice the construction of the imperatives in sentence two. There are three independent clauses with an understood subject (you). In this compound sentence, the coordinating conjunctions *or* and *but* effectively separate the three parts—the two that are compared and the one that contrasts.

Can you identify the dependent clause in the third sentence? Once again, it is led by

who, and its presence makes the sentence form complex. The subject of this sentence is the MASS NOUN **Sixty percent**, and the compound verb is **bring and plump**. Remember that the presence of compound verbs (or adverbs or adjectives) does not make the entire sentence compound in form; the conjunctions in this sentence connect only word groups and not clauses.

Take another look at that list of subordinating conjunctions on page 15. Thurber's seventh sentence uses one that deserves some extra consideration. The independent clause **They are afraid to ask for their money back** begins the sentence and can stand alone. It's followed by the dependent clause and its leader, *because*. This makes the sentence complex, and it is also important to note that, in formal writing, clauses beginning with *because*, if left on their own, are fragments, not complete thoughts. *Because* it's always a dependent clause, *because* must always be attached to an independent clause.

The final sentence has a *when* clause and a *who* clause that rely on the independent parts of the sentence for completeness: **when a mischievous puppy is returned to its former owner ... it behaves** and **person who brought it back**. The sentence itself can be divided into two parts, with the second part beginning with the coordinating conjunction *and*. Each section also has segments that can and cannot stand alone. The verdict? The form is compound-complex.

Imagine how the excerpt would have sounded if Thurber had used only simple sentences:

A drawing of Thurber by English artist Ronald Searle

Dog owners need to be warned to not give puppies away. Sell them. Keep them. Sixty percent of persons bring the dog back sooner or later and plump him into his former owner's lap. The people don't want the dog. You are stuck with him. New owners need to pay five or ten dollars for pups. They won't return them. They are afraid to ask for their money back. The returned puppy behaves beautifully.

over such a lifeless text, and as a good writer,

you don't want to risk that. Go for variety!

GO
FOR
VARIETY!

Life Time Investments

If someone told you there is nothing that young people can teach older people, how would you react? Maybe you've been the older one who has learned cooperation skills from a younger student just by spending time with him. Or perhaps you've shared your abilities with someone older than you are, such as finding information on an online site or developing an exercise technique. Or maybe you agree with the statement, feeling that older people always know more. Why do you feel that way? Write your opinion in simple, compound, and complex sentences. Include some dependent clauses, such as "When I was…," "Ever since the day…," and "If someone had told me…"

PUNCTUATION POINTERS

Constructing informative, readable sentences is not just about using different forms and types. Punctuation is also vitally important. English author Lynne Truss shares this insight in her book *Eats, Shoots & Leaves*: "Punctuation has been defined many ways…. But best of all, I think, is the simple advice given by the style book of a national newspaper: that punctuation is 'a courtesy designed to help readers to understand a story without stumbling.'"

We want to be correct, as well as polite. When we want to quote only part of an excerpt, we use an ellipsis (…) and place it after the end punctuation, as shown above. This shows we have left out some of the original work, but we have kept the main point intact. The choice of topic is something each author controls, but a text's readability has universal standards, and it depends on our having the good manners to learn how to punctuate correctly. Why? It's simple, really; we want somebody to read what we've written.

Some marks not mentioned previously—but which appear throughout this book—are colons and dashes. Sometimes a colon and a dash have similar uses, such as when the writer wants to stop the action in the middle of a sentence or give an example. Another function of the colon is to draw attention to what comes next, such as before lists and quotations. If the list is a short series, it makes sense to use a colon and keep the list within the sentence. But if you want to list several events or items, using a colon and setting the list in a vertical column will give the reader a chance to focus on each specific point. When a colon is used before a direct quotation, it has the effect of stopping the action of the sentence to prepare the reader for an important bit of knowledge. Look back through this book and see how many colons are used for this purpose—they're everywhere!

Sometimes using a colon is unnecessary. Avoid using it when the colon would separate a verb and its predicate nominatives {**The contestants** *were***: Barry, Ted, and Sean**}, when it would occur between a preposition and its object {**I found Internet sites** *for***: maps, weather, and news events**}, or when it would be after *such as* {**Before a race, many marathon runners eat carbohydrates,** *such as***: spaghetti, lasagna, and whole wheat grains**}. None of those examples needed a colon—the lists followed a verb (*were*), a preposition (*for*), and the phrase *such as*. Each colon was a disruption to the flow of information.

*An illustrated portrait of
Martin Luther King Jr.*

Semicolons are sometimes used instead of a comma and a coordinating conjunction to separate independent clauses in compound sentences. Instead of writing, **I've read the book, and I know how it ends,** you could write **I've read the book; I know how it ends.** Semicolons are also used for separating more than two independent clauses. We usually use a comma for a series, but when it's a series of clauses, semicolons are usually needed, as in this quote from Pope John XXIII: **See everything; overlook a great deal; correct a little.** The semicolon slows the writer's progress but indicates more is coming, and since it is more of a stop than a comma but less than a colon, it's a combination of those two punctuation marks. Semicolons are also used to separate series that already contain commas, such as this Swedish proverb: **Fear less, hope more; eat less, chew more; whine less, breathe more; talk less, say more; hate less, love more; and all good things are yours.**

The sight of a comma usually makes the reader pause. But the main thing is to have a good reason for using it in the first place. We have already established the relevance of using commas to divide independent clauses, to set apart the dependent ones, and to separate related things or people listed one after the other in a series. Now the list goes on.

To set off an introductory word or phrase, use a comma: **No, Sadie, I have not agreed to that. Sir, would you mind if I put you on hold for a moment? To Caesar, Brutus had seemed a friend.** A slight break in the sentence for a parenthetical element, as though we are using parentheses ( ), is also punctuated with commas. The sentence needs to make sense without the words in between the commas. In the following sentence, "indeed" is not necessary to make sense of the rest of the words: **That, indeed, was what his father was trying to avoid.**

To help the reader, two words that are spelled the same but have different grammatical functions within the sentence may be separated by a comma: **Whatever is, is good.** Likewise, if a potentially confusing reference needs to be clarified, such as when people's names might be misunderstood, use a comma to do it: **When our uncle called, Mary Jane answered the phone** versus **When our uncle called Mary, Jane answered the phone.** In contrast, sometimes a comma stands in place of a clearly understood word or group of words, as in **Fannie Lou Hamer and Martin Luther King both spoke openly about civil rights; one of them is honored by a national holiday, the other, not.** In this case, the final comma represents the word *is*.

TO COMMA

Appositives and commas sometimes seem at odds with one another. An appositive is a word or group of words that restates a noun, and it is set off by commas if it isn't essential to the meaning of the sentence. In the following sentence, "friend" is the appositive to "Tony": **Not even *Tony*, Wade's best *friend*, voted for him.** The appositive phrase, *Wade's best friend*, isn't essential information. Commas enclose it because we can take the phrase out of the sentence and still have a complete thought: **Not even Tony voted for him.** The tricky part of determining whether to comma or not to comma involves evaluating what is essential. If the word or group of words is absolutely necessary to the meaning of the sentence, leave out the commas: **Not even Wade's best friend Tony voted for him.** The one-word appositive, *Tony*, is essential to the explanation, so no commas are needed.

When two or more modifiers of equal importance come before a noun, a comma might be needed to separate them. Might? Yes, it depends on whether the adjectives are part of one unit or are separate descriptors. Try putting "and" in between them as a test. If they're individual and equal parts, yes, use a comma: **This is going to be a long, tedious project.** We can say "long *and* tedious." Yet in the sentence, **Grandma often wore a blue wool shawl,** "blue wool" makes up a single descriptor of "shawl." No comma is required.

Let's take a moment to examine how commas can send false signals. Stifle the urge to add a comma to pause or breathe when no standard reason for comma usage exists. The absence of a comma doesn't prevent the reader from pausing; it just leaves it up to the reader's interpretation. Foremost in the realm of comma "don'ts," never separate a subject from its verb, as in **The ball, went through the hoop!** or a verb from its object: **Poetic expression catches, the mind and hangs on.** Additionally, commas do not follow coordinating conjunctions and only precede them when they separate independent clauses. Instead of writing, **The dangers of smoking are well publicized but, millions of people still smoke,** move the comma before *but*. No comma is needed before the conjunction when you have only one main clause: **Millions of people know the dangers but smoke anyway.** Punctuation, especially correctly used commas, can make the difference in readers' abilities to understand our writing. A well-placed comma is an invaluable aid in helping us leave our mark.

OR NOT?

BUILD YOUR OWN SENTENCE
The Case for Commas

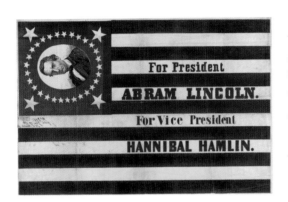

American writer Carl Sandburg's (1878–1967) biography, *Abraham Lincoln: The Prairie Years* (1926), shares tales of young Abe's increasing interest in the legal system. Commas have been removed from the following excerpt. Your task is to recopy it and put them where they belong. Hint: On two occasions, commas will replace words that are clearly understood. However, no commas are needed in the first 19 words. Find the 10 missing commas.

Afterwards on days when no passengers were in sight and it was "law day" at Squire Pate's down the river Abe would scull over and watch the witnesses the constables the Squire the machinery of law government justice.

The State of Indiana he learned was one thing and the State of Kentucky something else. A water line in the middle of a big river ran between them.

ANSWER KEY

Correct placement of the 10 commas (in red):

Afterwards on days when no passengers were in sight and it was "law day," at Squire Pate's down the river, Abe would scull over and watch the witnesses, the constables, the Squire, the machinery of law, government, justice.

The State of Indiana, he learned, was one thing, and the State of Kentucky, something else. A water line in the middle of a big river ran between them.

MARKS OF DISTINCTION

Writing a direct quotation involves reproducing the speaker's words exactly as they were spoken. Quotation marks surround the exact quote, such as **Winston Churchill stated, "Attitude is a little thing that makes a big difference."** We're quoting, or repeating other people's words, when we use quotation marks and actual dialogue in writing conversations between speakers. An indirect quote is a more informal paraphrase that doesn't use quotation marks, as in **Winston Churchill said that attitude is a little thing that makes a big difference.**

Being able to "hear" a character express him- or herself helps a reader form a better idea of who that character is. Such is the case with English author C. S. Lewis (1898–1963) and his use of dialogue in *The Lion, the Witch and the Wardrobe* (1950). Eight characters appear in the following excerpt: Aslan, the lion (the true ruler of the country of Narnia); Edmund, Peter, Susan, and Lucy (the children referred to as Edmund and "the others"); a leopard (a bodyguard); the dwarf (a messenger from the evil White Witch, now Queen of Narnia); and Mr. Beaver (one of Aslan's loyal subjects). Picture the scene in your mind as you hear each character speaking.

 "Here is your brother," [Aslan] said, "and— there is no need to talk to him about what is past."

Edmund shook hands with each of the others and said to each of them in turn, "I'm sorry," and everyone said, "That's all right." And then everyone wanted very hard to say something ... ordinary and natural—and of course no one could think of anything in the world to say. But before they had time to feel really awkward one of the leopards approached Aslan and said:

"Sire, there is a messenger from the enemy who craves audience."

"Let him approach," said Aslan.

The leopard went away and soon returned leading the Witch's Dwarf.

"What is your message, Son of Earth?" asked Aslan.

"The Queen of Narnia and Empress of the Lone Islands desires a safe conduct to come and speak with you," said the Dwarf, "on a matter which is as much to your advantage as to hers."

"Queen of Narnia, indeed!" said Mr. Beaver. "Of all the cheek—"

"Peace, Beaver," said Aslan. "All names will soon be restored to their proper owners.... Tell your mistress, Son of Earth, that I grant her safe conduct on condition that she leaves her wand behind her at that great oak."

This excerpt employs two formats in which quotations can be presented: 1) more than one speaker within the same paragraph and 2) a new paragraph with each change of speaker. The first way saves space and combines the topic with the related dialogue between Edmund and his siblings. The second clarifies the separate characters and their dispositions. That certainly is the case for revealing how Mr. Beaver feels about the Queen. It is the use of direct quotations—being able to hear the voices—that gives the reader the feeling of

Our word "apostrophe" comes from the Greek *apostrephein* for "turn away." We use apostrophes to create possessive forms and CONTRACTIONS. Possessives show ownership. The placement of the apostrophe depends on whether the noun that shows possession is singular or plural. Generally, if the noun is singular or if a plural noun does not end in -*s*, add '*s*: **the student's schedule, the children's playground**. If the noun is plural and already ends in *s*, add the apostrophe after the *s*: **the teachers' workroom, the**

FIRE!

being included in the action. Using quotation marks for what someone is thinking also helps the reader. If Mr. Beaver had thought, **"Queen of Narnia, indeed!"** and had not spoken it aloud, the words would still have been enclosed in quotation marks.

When a speaker is quoting another statement, the situation becomes a quote within a quote and needs to be marked differently. The double, or regular, quotation marks are still used around the main speaker's words, while the additional quote is enclosed in single quotation marks: **"When Julie saw the smoke,"** said Wally, **"she shouted, 'Fire!'"**

computers' hard drives. Thus, for plural possession, the apostrophe goes after the plural ending.

An apostrophe doesn't always mean the word is in a possessive form. It also shows where a letter or letters have been left out. In the sentence, **Everybody *who is* surprised raise your hand,** *who's* can be substituted for *who is*. While we usually avoid contractions in formal writing, correct colloquial, informal spoken usage requires an understanding of the original words that make up the contraction. See Table 1 for a list of common contractions and the words they replace.

CONTRACTIONS

CONTRACTION	ORIGINAL FORM	CONTRACTION	ORIGINAL FORM
aren't	are not	could've	could have
doesn't	does not	don't	do not
I'm	I am	isn't	is not
it's	it is/it has	let's	let us
mustn't	must not	she's	she is
there's	there is	they'd	they would/they had
they'll	they will	they're	they are
we're	we are	who's	who is
won't	will not	you're	you are

TABLE 1

MY MINE OUR OURS YOUR YOURS HIS HER HERS ITS THEIR THEIRS

Pronouns that are already possessive, such as *my*, *mine*, *our*, *ours*, *your*, *yours*, *his*, *her*, *hers*, *its*, *their*, and *theirs* should never have an *'s*. Take a look at this sentence: ***Her* fans saw every movie their favorite actress made.** To add an apostrophe to "her"—her's—would be a contraction for "her is," and that doesn't make any sense. "Her" and "hers" are already possessive; no apostrophe is needed.

When you want to add more words instead of contracting them, the hyphen (-) is a helpful mark. The test for using a hyphen resembles the comma test for equal modifiers before a noun: use a hyphen when inserting the word "and" between the two parts does not make sense. If you attend school full time, you may describe yourself as **a full-time student,** right? Full-time doesn't mean a full *and* time student, so the hyphen is fine. But a bright young lady is both bright *and* young; there's no need to connect the two parts. Skip the hyphen.

What deserves the hyphen? These do: IMPROVISED COMPOUND words {a **never-say-die** attitude} {a **make-believe** world}; single capital letters joined to nouns {**X-ray** department} {an **A-flat** major scale}; relationship compounds {**brothers-in-law**} {**parent-teacher** conferences}; fractions if they are spelled out {**two-thirds**} {one and **five-eighths**}; a numbered figure and its unit of measurement {**2-liter** bottle} {**8-foot** boards}; nouns that use *ex* {**ex-girlfriend**} and *self* {**self-respect**}; adjectives that need to avoid

doubling a vowel or tripling a consonant {**semi-independent**} {**bell-like**}; words that could otherwise be misunderstood or mispronounced {**re-cover** the chair as distinguished from *recover* from an illness} {a potluck supper is a **co-op**, not a coop}. When in doubt, grab a dictionary and look it up.

The basic rules of punctuation haven't changed much since English author Charles Dickens (1812–70) wrote *Great Expectations* (1860–61). In the following excerpt, the main character, seven-year-old Pip, narrates a scene in which guests come to his sister's (Mrs. Joe's) house for Christmas dinner.

Charles Dickens, photographed in the 1860s

"I opened the door to the company, first to Mr. Wopsle, next to Mr. and Mrs. Hubble, and last of all to Uncle Pumblechook. (I was not allowed to call him "uncle," under the severest penalties.)

"Mrs. Joe," said Uncle Pumblechook—a large, hard-breathing, middle-aged, slow man, with a mouth like a fish, dull staring eyes, and sandy hair standing upright on his head, so that he looked as if he had just been all but choked, and had that moment come to—"I have brought you as the compliments of the season—I have brought you, mum, a bottle of sherry wine—and I have brought you, mum, a bottle of port wine." Every Christmas Day he presented himself, as a profound novelty, with exactly the same words, and carrying the two bottles like dumbbells."

Let's see how punctuation aids this excerpt. Commas in the first sentence separate the series of appositives for **the company,** introducing them to the reader by name: Mr. Wopsle, Mr. and Mrs. Hubble, and Uncle Pumblechook. The parentheses show that Pip's explanation of Pumblechook was not part of the story he was telling (*I* **was not allowed to call him "uncle,"**…) but was part of his world. Why put quotation marks around *uncle*? That's to set off the word being used as a word. The comma following *uncle* sets the beginning clause apart from the PREPOSITIONAL PHRASE. Next come the quotation marks for Pumblechook's exact words of presentation of the wine bottles to Mrs. Joe—a direct quotation. In the midst of his speech is Pip's description of Pumblechook himself, the hyphenated compounds (**hard-breathing, middle-aged**) as adjectives of equal importance, framed in commas so the reader can easily distinguish between them. The entire description of the boorish uncle is also set apart for emphasis with dashes. And using **mum** twice as a noun of address is accented by the commas. The final sentence uses commas to separate the series of phrases. That is quite a punctuation review!

The author also gives us a review of sentence types. Periods are effective stops after each of the four declarative sentences—three simple sentences surrounding the one compound-complex (compound with the two

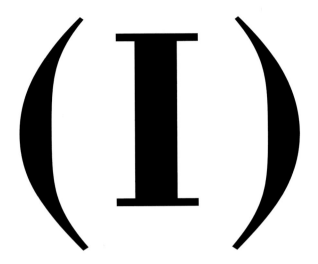

I have brought you independent clauses; complex with the **that he looked** and **if he had** dependent clauses). Dickens's tale is narrated from Pip's viewpoint, and in this excerpt the reader sees what Pip sees, hears what Pip hears, and knows how Pip feels about experiencing exactly the same routine every Christmas Day.

Writing precise sentences takes practice. Comprehending correct punctuation involves *using* it and, at times, coming to its defense. Simply knowing there's a difference in sentence forms and functions—differentiating the imperative from the interrogative, the declarative from the exclamatory, and all from simple to compound-complex—will serve you well. What's more, a proficiency in punctuation marks will ensure that your words fall into place grammatically without causing your reader to trip. So make your mark with confidence, and write well!

Scenes from the Academy Award-winning 1946 film version of **Great Expectations**

BUILD YOUR OWN SENTENCE
Odd One Out

Have you ever played the game "Two Truths and a Lie"? The object is to fool someone else by what you've written—two things that are correct and one that isn't. Pick a partner and play the game with apostrophes. For example, you might write these phrases on your paper: "the five Bergman cousin's houses," "the Maeders' children," and "the student's backpack." Only two are grammatically correct. Do you know why the first one isn't? Here's a hint: for plural possession, the apostrophe goes after the plural noun. In this case, the plural is *cousins*, so the plural possessive is *cousins'*. If you get stuck for ideas, you may also use contractions (listed in Table 1) and possessive pronouns to make a few phrases. Take turns quizzing with your friend. Be sure your errors are intentional!

GLOSSARY

contractions: shortened forms of a word or group of words, with the missing letters usually marked by an apostrophe

improvised compound: a hyphenated word created for a specific use from two or more separate words

interjection: a part of speech that expresses an exclamation of sudden feeling

main clause: a group of words with a subject and a verb that makes sense by itself and to which other dependent clauses may be connected

mass noun: in English, usually a noun that lacks a plural in ordinary usage and is not used with articles (*a*, *an*, or *the*)

modifiers: words or groups of words that describe, limit, or qualify another word

narration: a written or spoken account of past events

objects: persons or things to which a specified action is directed

part of speech: the class or category into which a word may be grouped according to its form changes and its grammatical function; in English, the main parts of speech are verbs, nouns, pronouns, adjectives, adverbs, prepositions, conjunctions, and interjections

predicate: the part of a clause or sentence containing a verb and stating something about the subject

predicate nominative: a word in the nominative (naming) case that occurs in the part of the sentence containing the verb; it completes a linking verb and renames the subject

prepositional phrase: a group of words consisting of a preposition (*at, by, of, to,* etc.), its object, and any modifiers

punctuation: marks used to provide meaning and separate elements within sentences, such as periods, commas, question marks, exclamation points, semicolons, colons, hyphens, and parentheses

relative pronoun: a noun substitute, such as *which, who,* or *that*, used to introduce a subordinate clause

sentence: a unit of expression that contains a subject and a verb and expresses a complete, independent thought

subordinate clauses: groups of words with a subject and verb that cannot stand alone; also known as dependent clauses

SELECTED BIBLIOGRAPHY

The Chicago Manual of Style. 15th ed. Chicago: The University of Chicago Press, 2003.

Hodges, John C., Winifred B. Horner, Suzanne S. Webb, and Robert K. Miller. *Harbrace College Handbook.* 13th ed. Fort Worth, Tex.: Harcourt Brace College Publishers, 1998.

Lederer, Richard, and Richard Dowis. *Sleeping Dogs Don't Lay: Practical Advice for the Grammatically Challenged.* New York: St. Martin's Press, 1999.

O'Conner, Patricia T. *Woe Is I: The Grammarphobe's Guide to Better English in Plain English.* New York: Riverhead Books, 2004.

———. *Woe Is I Jr.: The Younger Grammarphobe's Guide to Better English.* New York: G. P. Putnam's Sons, 2007.

Strunk, William, and E. B. White. *The Elements of Style.* 4th ed. New York: Longman Publishers, 2000.

Truss, Lynne. *Eats, Shoots & Leaves: The Zero Tolerance Approach to Punctuation.* New York: Gotham Books, 2004.

Walsh, Bill. *The Elephants of Style: A Trunkload of Tips on the Big Issues and Gray Areas of Contemporary American English.* New York: McGraw-Hill, 2004.

INDEX